TABLE OF CONT

CW00503314

Chim Chim Cher-ee

(from Mary Poppins)

Words & Music by Richard M. Sherman &
Robert B. Sherman

03

04

Much slower

A tempo ♩ = 168

(with piano)

f

A tempo ♩ = 160

rit.

(with bass clarinet)

mp   *p*

rit. poco a poco

f

molto rit.

A tempo ♩ = 144

ff

05

Hopelessly Devoted To You

(from Grease)

Words & Music by John Farrar

07

Music Box Dance

(from The Snowman)

Music by Howard Blake

Tempo di valse

Violin

09

Dance Of The Snowmen

(from The Snowman)

Music by Howard Blake

11

(I've Had) The Time Of My Life

Words & Music by Frankie Previte, John
DeNicola & Donald Markowitz

to Coda ⊕

mp animato

cresc. poco a poco

D.S. al Coda   Coda

mf

3

3

3

3

2   Instrumental break   **7**

mf ——— *f*

Softly

synth./guitar/brass cue   *p dolce*

4 3

4 3   *4*

mf   *3*

With a heavy beat

4   *3*

f   *3*

Repeat to fade

3

14

A Love Before Time
(from Crouching Tiger, Hidden Dragon)

Words & Music by James Schamus,
Tan Dun & Jorge Calandrelli

Mothersbaugh's Canon

(from The Royal Tenenbaums)

Mark Mothersbaugh

Pelagia's Song
(from Captain Corelli's Mandolin)

Stephen Warbeck

Queen Of My Heart

Words & Music by John McLaughlin, Wayne
Hector, Steve Mac & Steve Robson

mf folkishly
ornamented

cresc.

f

23

When You Believe
(from The Prince Of Egypt)

Words & Music by
Stephen Schwartz

Slowly

25

Goldfinger

Words by Leslie Bricusse & Anthony
Newley Music by John Barry

Raiders March

(from Raiders Of The Lost Ark)

Music by John Williams

With movement

The Heart Asks Pleasure First: The Promise/The Sacrifice (from The Piano)

Music by Michael Nyman

Moderate tempo, flowing

30

31

Theme from E.T. - The Extra-Terrestrial

Music by John Williams

Yumeji's Theme
(from 'In The Mood For Love')

Shigeru Umebayashi

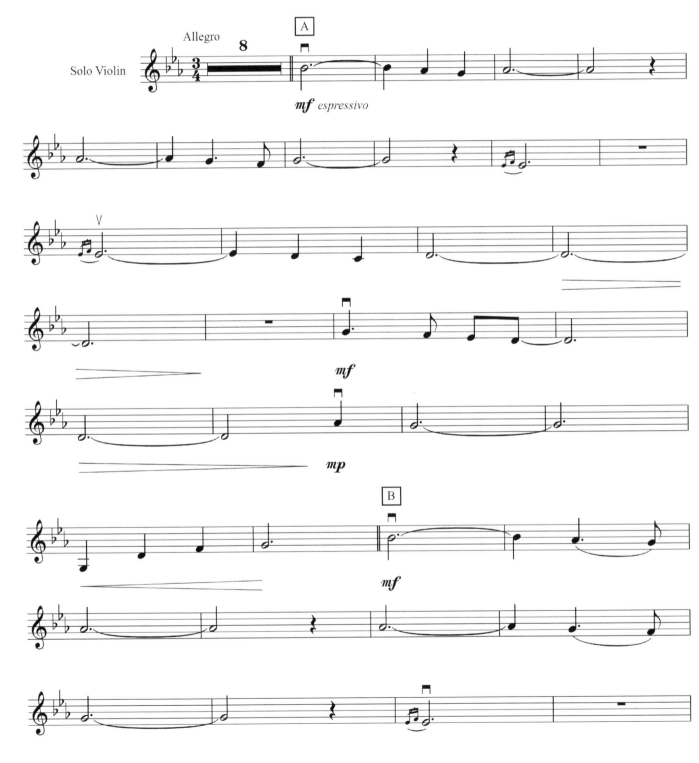

Moon River

Words by Johnny Mercer Music by
Henry Mancin

Suddenly
(from Les Miserables The Movie)

Music by Claude-Michel Schönberg
Lyrics by Herbert Kretzmer and Alain Boublil

Skyfall

(from the Motion Picture Skyfall)

Words & Music by Adele Adkins & Paul Epworth

(brass cue)

41

I See Fire (from The Hobbit)

Words & Music by Ed Sheeran

44

Easter Parade

Words and Music by
IRVING BERLIN

Under The Sea
(from The Little Mermaid)

Music by ALAN MENKEN
Lyrics by HOWARD ASHMAN

48

D.S. al Coda

Hakuna Matata (from The Lion King)

Music by ELTON JOHN
Lyrics by TIM RICE

The Bare Necessities

Words and Music
byTERRY GILKYSON

The Brady Bunch

Words and Music by
SHERWOOD SCHWARTZ
and FRANK DEVOL

Born Free

Words by DON BLACK
Music by JOHN BARRY

The Odd Couple

By NEAL HEFTI

The John Dunbar Theme

By JOHN BARRY

Forrest Gump - Main Title
(Feather Theme)

Music by ALAN SILVESTRI

Love Theme From "St. Elmo's Fire"

Words and Music by DAVID FOSTER

The Climb
(from Hannah Montana: The Movie)

Words and Music by JESSI ALEXANDER and JON MABE

Mission: Impossible Theme

By Lalo Schifrin
Arranged by Lindsey Stirling and The Piano Guys

Pokemon Theme

Words and Music by T. Loeffler and J.
SieglerArranged by Lindsey Stirling and Kirt
Hugo SchneiderTamara Loeffler & John Siegler

64

Let It Go (from Frozen)

Music and Lyrics by Kristen Anderson-Lopezand Robert Lopez
Arranged by Al van der Beek,Jon Schmidt and Steven Sharp Nelson

65

The Godfather (Love Theme)

By NINO ROTA

Lava (from Lava)

Music and Lyrics by JAMES FORD MURPHY

Swinging On A Star

Words by JOHNNY BURKE
Music by JIMMY VAN HEUSEN

Shallow (from A Star Is Born)

Words and Music by STEFANI
GERMANOTTA,MARK RONSON, ANDREW
WYATTand ANTHONY ROSSOMANDO

Mia & Sebastian's Theme

(from La La Land)

Music by JUSTIN HURWITZ

Never Enough

(from The Greatest Showman)

Words and Music by BENJ PASEK and JUSTIN PAUL

Rewrite The Stars
(from The Greatest Showman)

Words and Music by BENJ PASEK and JUSTIN PAUL

Gabriel's Oboe

Words and Music by ENNIO MORRICONE

A Million Dreams

(from The Greatest Showman)

Words and Music by BENJ PASEK and JUSTIN PAUL

Over The Rainbow

(from The Wizard Of Oz)

Music by HAROLD ARLEN\
Lyric by E.Y. "YIP" HARBURG

You're Welcome (from Moana)

Lin-Manuel Miranda

Believe (from The Polar Express)

Words and Music by GLEN BALLARD
and ALAN SILVESTRI

City Of Stars (from La La Land)

Music by JUSTIN HURWITZ
Lyrics by BENJ PASEK & JUSTIN PAUL

Somewhere In My Memory

John Williams

Breaking Free

Words & Music by Jamie Houston

molto rit.

Mrs Robinson

Words & Music by Paul Simon

A DREAM IS A WISH YOUR HEART MAKES

"Words and Music by MACK DAVID,
AL HOFFMAN and JERRY LIVINGSTON"

WHEN WILL MY LIFE BEGIN?

Music by ALAN MENKEN
Lyrics by GLENN SLATER

Slowly, freely
♩ = 88

Printed in Great Britain
by Amazon

28270880R00053